THE HUBBLE SPACE TELESCOPE

A TRUE BOOK

by

**Diane M. and
Paul P. Sipiera**

Children's Press®
A Division of Grolier Publishing

New York London Hong Kong Sydney
Danbury, Connecticut

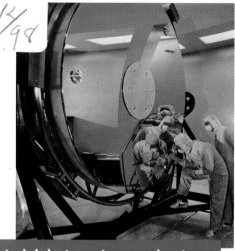

Hubble's mirror during construction

Subject Consultant
Peter Goodwin
*Science Department Chairman
Kent School, Kent, CT*

Reading Consultant
Linda Cornwell
*Learning Resource Consultant
Indiana Department
of Education*

Authors' Dedication:
To Loren W. Acton—
astronomer, astronaut,
and good friend

Library of Congress Cataloging-in-Publication Data

Sipiera, Diane M.
    The Hubble Space Telescope / by Diane M. Sipiera and Paul P. Sipiera.
    p. cm. — (A true book)
    Includes bibliographical references and index.
    Summary: Describes how the Hubble Space Telescope was placed into
orbit and how it has brought us more information about outer space.
    ISBN 0-516-20442-4 (lib. bdg.)   0-516-26266-1 (pbk.)
    1. Hubble Space Telescope (Spacecraft) —Juvenile literature. 2. Outer
space—Exploration—Juvenile literature. [1. Hubble Space Telescope
(Spacecraft) 2. Outer space—Exploration.] I. Sipiera, Paul P. II. Title. III.
Series.
QB500.268.S46 1997
522'.2919—dc21

96-29830
CIP
AC

Contents

People have always been curious about the night sky.

History of the Telescope

For thousands of years, people have looked at the night sky. Many objects caught their eye. The Moon changed its shape, planets moved against a background of stars, and stars changed position from season to season. People wanted to learn more about the sky.

The view of the night sky changed after the invention of the telescope. In 1608, a Dutch lensmaker named Hans Lippershey was working with two lenses. By chance, he placed one lens in front of the other and saw an image larger than the one he saw without the lens. This accident led to the invention of the telescope.

In 1609, the Italian scientist Galileo Galilei heard about the telescope. He quickly made

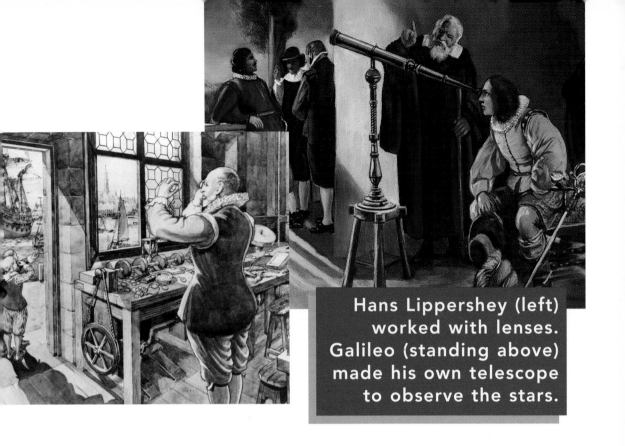

Hans Lippershey (left)
worked with lenses.
Galileo (standing above)
made his own telescope
to observe the stars.

one for himself to study the
stars. Galileo found that there
were many more stars than
anyone had imagined. What
he learned about the universe
changed astronomy forever.

Different Kinds of Telescopes

The kind of telescope used by Galileo is called a refracting telescope. It has a large lens, called the objective lens, placed at one end of a tube. This lens collects light from a star or a planet. At the other end of the tube is a smaller

Galileo's telescope

lens. This lens, called the magnifying lens, makes an object look bigger. Sometimes, other lenses are placed between the objective and magnifying lenses to improve the image.

Refracting and Reflecting Telescopes

A **refracting telescope** has an objective lens on the end of a tube. The light collected by this lens goes through a magnifying lens at the other end of the tube.

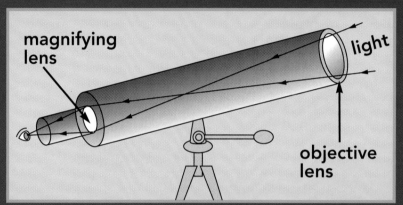

magnifying lens

light

objective lens

One end of a **reflecting telescope** is open to let in light. When light enters, it hits a mirror at the other end of the tube. This light reflects up to a smaller mirror and then onto a magnifying lens.

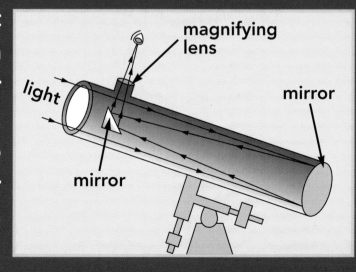

magnifying lens

light

mirror

mirror

A second kind of telescope, called a reflecting telescope, was invented by Sir Isaac Newton in 1668. It uses a mirror instead of a lens to collect light. One end

Newton studied the way light reflects.

of the telescope is left open to let in the light. When light enters the telescope, it hits a mirror at the other end. The light then reflects back up the telescope to a smaller mirror and then onto a magnifying lens. In the years since Newton invented the reflecting telescope, its design has been improved.

Both refracting and reflecting telescopes are used in astronomy, but almost all the world's observatories use the reflecting telescope. It is less expensive and can be made larger than a refracting telescope.

The visible light given off by stars and planets is not the only

An image of the Sun
(right) as seen from an
X-ray telescope (left)

form of energy that can be collected by a telescope. There
are special telescopes that
look for infrared or heat energy. Others search for X rays or
other high-energy sources.

Telescopes in Space

One of an astronomer's biggest problems is having to look at the stars through the earth's atmosphere. The atmosphere makes the sky appear blue during the day and makes stars seem to twinkle at night. It also makes the stars and planets look fuzzy when seen through a telescope.

For hundreds of years, astronomers dreamed of having a telescope above the atmosphere. The best they could do was build their observatories on top of the highest mountains, where the air was thinner and the view was clearer. The atmosphere was still a problem, however. As people became more interested in exploring space

Observatories, such as this one in Arizona (left), are often built on high mountains. The telescope in this Hawaiian observatory (right) has a mirror 33 feet (10 meters) wide.

in the 1950s, astronomers hoped to have telescopes orbiting the earth. They also hoped to have an observatory on the Moon.

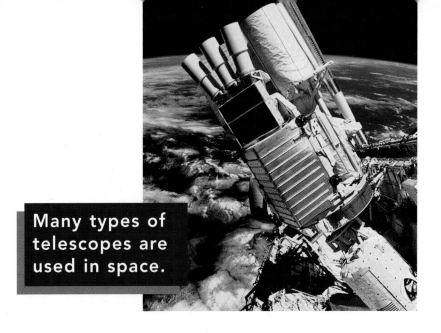

Many types of telescopes are used in space.

Today, many types of telescopes are used in space to bring us clear pictures from above the earth's atmosphere. When scientists started to develop the Hubble Space Telescope to orbit the earth, they decided to make it a reflecting telescope.

The Hubble Space Telescope

After more than twenty years, and with the help and hard work of more than ten thousand people, the Hubble Space Telescope was finally ready. It was released into orbit from the space shuttle *Discovery* on April 24, 1990.

It was named after Edwin P. Hubble, a famous American astronomer.

The Hubble Space Telescope is huge compared to other satellites. It weighs 25,000 pounds (11,340 kilograms) and is 43 feet (13 meters) long, about as big as a school bus. Its mirror, which collects light from stars, is 96 inches (240 centimeters) across. Hubble was designed to observe objects fifty times fainter than can be seen from Earth.

Edwin P. Hubble

Edwin P. Hubble (1889–1953) was an American astronomer. He worked with reflecting telescopes at the Mount Wilson Observatory near Pasadena, California. Hubble made many important discoveries. He was one of the first scientists to show that distant galaxies move away from the earth, which means that the universe is expanding. Before Hubble, most scientists thought that the universe stayed the same size.

Astronomers hoped the telescope would find objects that date back to the beginning of the universe.

Several other instruments are built into the Hubble Space

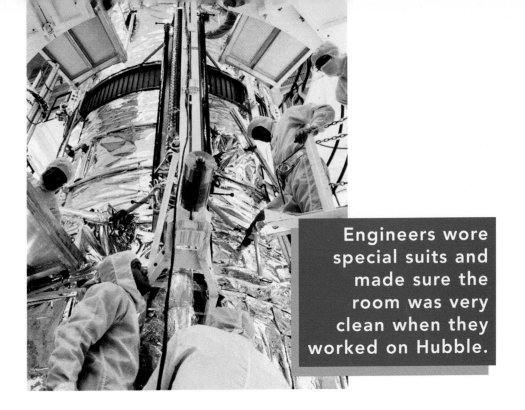

Telescope, each about the size of a telephone booth. These instruments include two spectrographs that help scientists study light and two cameras designed to observe planets and very faint objects.

The telescope is designed so that it can be repaired in space. All the scientific equipment on the telescope can be taken off and replaced by astronauts without bringing the telescope back to Earth.

A Problem with Hubble

Once the Hubble Space Telescope was placed into orbit, astronomers were eager to use it. They performed several tests to see if the telescope worked properly, but no one expected any serious trouble. When the first pictures were taken, however, it was

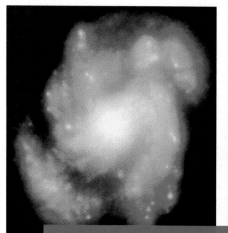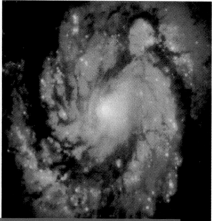

Hubble's first images looked blurry (left). Scientists needed to find solutions to get clearer pictures (right).

clear that something was very wrong. The pictures were blurred. Many people thought the telescope was useless, but the scientists would not give up.

First, the scientists tried to find the problem. Soon, engineers discovered that the telescope's mirror had been made incorrectly. The light collected by the telescope could not be focused.

Once scientists understood the problem that caused the poor focus, they developed computer programs that corrected the fuzzy images. The results were remarkable.

This was possible because the Hubble Space Telescope does not take photographs in the same way as a telescope

Hubble's images are sent to computers at the Space Telescope Science Institute at Johns Hopkins University in Baltimore, Maryland.

on Earth. Images from the telescope go into a computer and are sent by radio to Earth. Here, another computer makes the images into pictures.

Astronauts to the Rescue

Although the new computer programs improved the images Hubble was sending, the basic problem could not be fixed from Earth. Since the telescope was designed to be fixed by astronauts, a rescue mission was planned. The

29

Astronauts prepared to fix Hubble in space by training underwater.

astronauts would replace one of the original mirrors in Hubble with a new one to correct the focus problem.

The job of repairing the Hubble Space Telescope was not easy. In December 1993, the space shuttle *Endeavour* and its crew flew to the rescue. First, they caught up with the telescope in orbit and captured it. Then they brought it into the shuttle bay where the astronauts began repairs. The shuttle bay doors were open, so the astronauts had to leave the shuttle cabin and make five

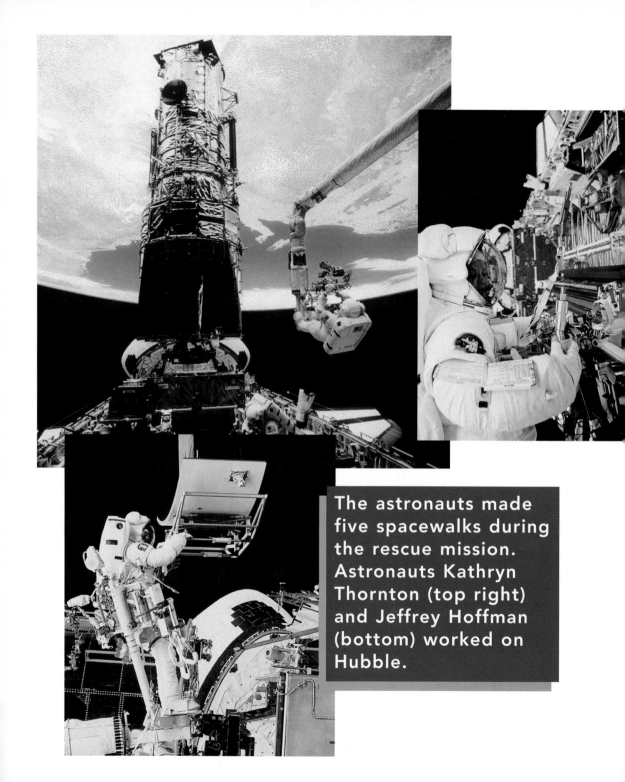

The astronauts made five spacewalks during the rescue mission. Astronauts Kathryn Thornton (top right) and Jeffrey Hoffman (bottom) worked on Hubble.

spacewalks to Hubble to do their work.

After three years in space, Hubble needed a lot of attention. Not only did the astronauts fix the focus, but they solved several other problems as well. When they finished their repairs, Hubble was a much better telescope.

The Hubble Space Telescope was serviced again in February 1997. The crew of the space shuttle *Discovery* replaced

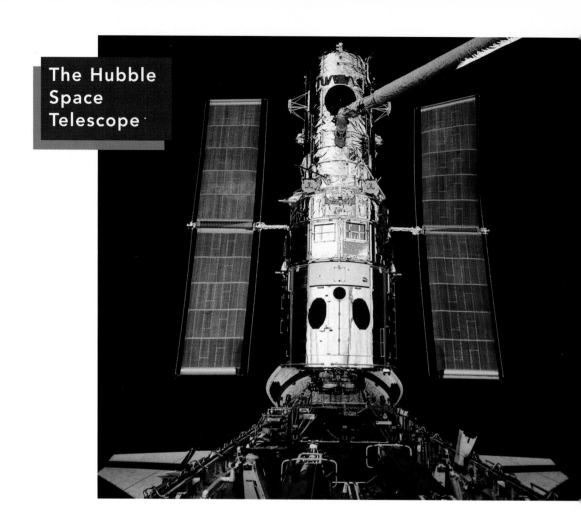

some of Hubble's instruments
with newer versions that could
collect more information and
light.

Hubble Discoveries

Since its launch, the Hubble Space Telescope has provided astronomers with many exciting discoveries. One of the earliest Hubble images showed the structure of galaxies. With even the best telescopes on Earth, the spiral structure of many galaxies

Many galaxies have a spiral shape.

cannot be seen. The fine detail of the Hubble images also shows that most galaxies are much larger than scientists had thought.

Astronomers have been waiting a long time to see a

black hole. Hubble's images of a giant galaxy called M87 show possible proof of a giant black hole at its center. Black holes can also form as individual stars die. Hubble is looking for them, too.

In 1994, a comet hit the planet Jupiter. Almost every large telescope on Earth observed the impact, but Hubble, out in space, had the best view. It sent wonderful images back to Earth shortly after the comet hit. The

Hubble provided scientists with clear pictures of a comet (above) hitting Jupiter in 1994. The brown spots are where the comet hit the planet (right).

images helped scientists understand what happens when a comet hits a planet.

Hubble has also recorded several volcanic eruptions on Jupiter's moon, Io. But Jupiter is not the only planet

Hubble was able to take pictures of Pluto and its moon Charon. Pluto is the smallest planet in the solar system.

observed by Hubble. It also looks at the clouds of Saturn and Neptune and watches weather conditions on Mars. In addition, Hubble took the best pictures ever seen of Pluto and its moon, Charon.

"The Pillars of Creation" (left) is the name given to one of Hubble's most incredible photos of clouds of gas and dust.

Some of Hubble's most beautiful pictures are of clouds of gas and dust. Within these clouds, stars are forming. Perhaps some of these stars will be orbited by planets someday—and some of these planets may be able to support life.

Hubble's Photo Gallery

The Hubble Space Telescope's pictures of stars, galaxies, clouds of dust and gases, and planet storms have helped scientists discover many secrets of the universe.

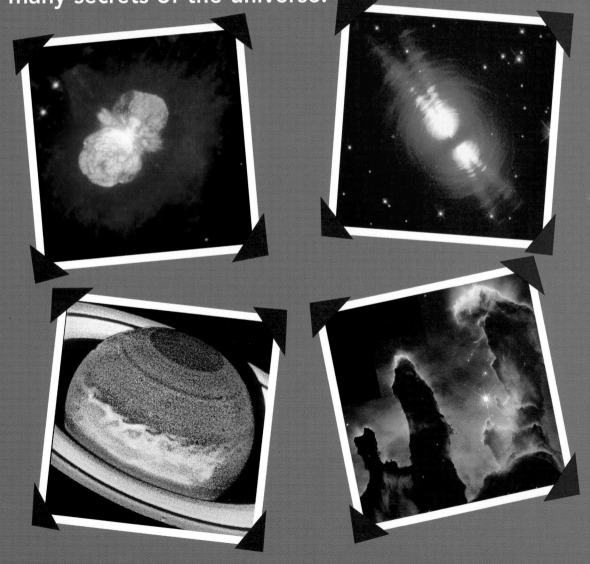

The Value of Hubble

The Hubble Space Telescope has given astronomers the view of space they always wanted. With a telescope high above the atmosphere, scientists are learning much about the secrets of the universe. And there is still more to discover.

A scientist watches closely to see the amazing pictures Hubble will send him next.

The Hubble Space Telescope is just the first step toward bringing the study of astronomy into space. Someday soon, astronomers may have an observatory on an international space station or on the Moon. One can only wonder what they will find from there.

To Find Out More

Here are more places to learn about space exploration:

 **Books**

 **Organizations**

Hitzeroth, Deborah. **Telescopes: Searching the Heavens.** Lucent Books, 1991.

Scott, Elaine. **Adventure in Space: The Flight to Fix the Hubble.** Hyperion, 1994.

Sipiera, Paul P. **Comets and Meteor Showers.** Children's Press, 1997.

Sipiera, Paul P. **Galaxies.** Children's Press, 1997.

Vogt, Gregory. **The Hubble Space Telescope.** Millbrook, 1992.

Astronomical Society of the Pacific
390 Ashton Avenue
San Francisco, CA 94112
(415) 337-1100
http://www.aspsky.org

NASA Teacher Resource Center
Mail Stop 8-1
NASA Lewis Research Center
21000 Brookpark Road
Cleveland, OH 44135
(216) 433-4000

National Air and Space Museum
Smithsonian Institution
601 Independence Ave. SW
Washington, DC 20560
(202) 357-1300

Online Sites

The Children's Museum of Indianapolis

*http://childrensmuseum.org/
sq1.htm*

Visit the SpaceQuest Planetarium to see what it has to offer, including a view of this month's night sky. It can connect you to other astronomy Web sites, too.

History of Space Exploration

*http://bang.lanl.gov/
solarsys/history.htm*

This site has a helpful timeline of space exploration and tells the history of the spacecraft and astronauts.

Kid's Space

*http://liftoff.msfc.nasa.gov/
kids/welcome.html*

Space exploration is really fun at this Web site. Find out how much you would weigh on the Moon, play games, solve puzzles, take quizzes, read stories, and look at the gallery of pictures drawn by kids. Find out how you can post a drawing online, too!

NASA Home Page

http://www.nasa.gov

Visit NASA to access information about its exciting history and present resources.

The Nine Planets

*http://seds.lpl.arizona.edu/
nineplanets/nineplanets/
nineplanets.html*

Take a multimedia tour of the solar system and all of its planets and moons.

Space Telescope Science Institute

http://www.stsci.edu/

The Space Telescope Science Institute is in charge of operating the Hubble Space Telescope. Visit this site to see pictures of the telescope's outer-space view.

Important Words

astronomy the study of the stars and planets

atmosphere layers of gases that surround a planet

galaxy billions of stars held together by gravity

infrared heat energy that cannot be seen

lens a curved piece of clear material that bends light to form an image

observatory a building where astronomers use a telescope to study the sky

orbit the path an object travels around a planet or star

satellite an object that orbits the earth

universe all the stars, galaxies, planets, and atoms that exist

X rays high-energy particles that cannot be seen

Index

M eet the Authors

Paul and Diane Sipiera are a husband and wife who share interests in nature and science. Paul is a professor of geology and astronomy at William Rainey Harper College in Palatine, Illinois. He is a member of the Explorers Club, the New Zealand Antarctic Society, and was a member of the United States Antarctic Research Program. Diane is the director of education for the Planetary Studies Foundation of Algonquin, Illinois. She also manages and operates the STARLAB planetarium program for her local school district.

When they are not studying or teaching science, Diane and Paul can be found enjoying their farm in Galena, Illinois, with their daughters, Andrea, Paula Frances, and Carrie Ann.